Swallowing Stones

3-11-23

Swallowing Stones

Poems by

Lisa St. John

Richard—
Thanks for your
poetry and support.

[signature]

Cover design by Shay Culligan
Cover image by Aaron Burden via Unsplash

ISBN: 978-1-63980-249-4

Kelsay Books
502 South 1040 East, A-119
American Fork, Utah 84003
Kelsaybooks.com

Dedicated to my sisters, who see my light.

Acknowledgments

Thank you to the following editors of publications in which these poems first appeared. Thank you to the Stone Ridge Library Writer's Group, who helped give birth to my poems. I also thank the Poetry Witch Community for their fine-tuning and my International Women's Writing Guild sisters for lifting me up.

2elizabeths: "Peter Pan's Madrigal," "Where is Ophelia's Mother?" "What I Want," "The Whens of Now," "Listen"

Ask For Arts Poetic License Exhibition: "Día de los Muertos"

Chronogram: "Saturday Poetry Workshop"

The Ekphrastic Review: "On Magritte's *The Voice of Blood*"

Entropy Magazine: "Forgive Me, But I Wasn't Feeling So Civil"

Eyedrum Periodically: "Not If But When," "Who Gets to Be You, Now?" "Why We Are Here"

Fish Anthology: "Mowing the Lawn"

Hudson Valley Writers Guild: "Pieta"

Light: "Of Light and Mornings"

Mid-Hudson Arts Poets Respond to Art: "Rule of Thumb"

The Poet's Billow: "There Must Be a Science to This"

Ponderings: "Dressing Mom," "Desert," "Dinner"

Contents

III

I

Día de los Muertos

Come home.

Afraid that building an *offrenda*
would wake you
from some sacred silence, I mixed new
mortar instead.

Adding sunrises from Puerto Peñesco,
dolphins too;
I mixed in a bit of cement
and a touch of rebar for remembrance.

Perhaps this *retablo* will offer me guidance
in the sacrilege of hope.

Then again,
I'm no painter.

Merging
San Miguel de Allende's cobbled hills
against Pacific fierceness
from Los Cabos,
I sprinkle with migrating whales.

I can wish for the impossible here,
in our intimate
Sonoran skies
Oaxacan hills . . .

I reach into this batter
and taste.

I swallow stones.

Dressing Mom

Soft as new skin, pliable as silk,
the casing of her bony arms
slide into the bra straps.
After the hospital, at this age,
I cannot help but wonder why she bothers.

Only whores go without bras.

Earlier, helping her wash,
I sponge underneath and around
the long empty breasts that fed five children.
I hold her as she washes the feathery gray pudendum,
the mysterious labia; origin places.

I hate for you to see me like this.

I ask
which shirt she wants to wear,
and she smiles up at me
grateful and gentle.
Nothing like her mothering years.

Then, the hard core of self-preservation
created us both. Born out of its hard shell
with eyes open and screaming, we traded combat secrets
and realized we were both
alone in this war.

How long can you stay this time?
We could go to that bookstore you like.

What
would have happened
if I had loved her like this before?
Loved her smooth tan skin
before the rice paper wrinkles?

Hatred is just the awkward side of love.

Headless Women

For The Winged Victory of Samothrace *c. 190 B.C*

I didn't know who you were
when I carefully cut you out of the art history book—
such sacrilege—
push-pinned you to my teenage wall.

Your ocean-drenched belly, graceful and precise
proud breasts brazen,
chest forward . . . a delicacy of stone in motion.

I was far from finished,
but the chisel
had already left its marks.

You were not left to the imagination. You
once had a head. *If only I had no head,*
too young to consider hope. But,
you, voluptuous, wind-swept—you
were unsheltered, you survived.

I learned the language of your followers much later:
Hellenistic, contour, sinuous. I too
wanted to be held by the wind.

They imagine your head, your arms,
but who needs arms when you have wings?

A fearless fluttering of grey marble, such movement in stillness,
you are a celebration of the body's force.
Sister of strength, daughter of Styx,
I cried in absurd supplication
when I saw you for the first time, in person,
in stone, in light.

They searched in vain for your head.
They remodel, surmise, envision, reconstruct what
Victory must have looked like;
what terrifying countenance they concoct. But,

your face . . . my face.

There Must Be a Science to This

There must be a science to this—an improbable equation
or a Fibonacci sequence that refuses
to spiral into madness.
These are not my memories. I reject this gift.

When I was thirteen they put us in a P.O.W. camp . . .

Perhaps a little of this drink and some of those pills
and a few hits, some greedy sex, and—
I will be fine. I will not accept your nightmares
regardless of the remuneration offered.
I refuse this guilt you silently pronounce as mine.

I read that suicide is for those people too gentle for this world.

It must be the equal sign that's missing.
Either that or your forgiveness.
I never was any good at math,
where the answers are always the same.
I waited for the new and improved mom
to come back from the hospital
each time, but the solution
must have been made of imaginary numbers.

Your situation had too many variables for me
to try and balance. But your stories stayed
with me as memories of things I had never seen . . .
There must be a science to this—
a sign, a symbol, a proof worth solving.

When I was fifteen a soldier took me to a hotel room and . . .

I will find the puzzle's missing piece
and eat it in remembrance of you.
I was not made to be complete.

The Whens of Now

When the gloaming begins
and the sky becomes a Turner painting,
when the air smells of fallen leaves
and cut grass,
when crickets serenade the last
of the fireflies—that now.

When hero-bats flood
the dwindling horizon light, and frogs
are in a brief conclave with sleepy bees,
when trees turn silhouette from the bottom up—

When just before the darkening oranges
take over for their 15 seconds of fame
and we could be in the Sedona Red Rocks
or in a field of Van Gogh's St Remy sunflowers
when we sit on the rooftop
in San Miguel de Allende drinking wine,

when, when, when this is now—if only for a moment. It was.

Oh, here comes the past tense again. Not yet.

Mowing the Lawn

You would hate the way I mow the lawn—my line-ish things, my
lack of symmetry, my
desire to go over the same spot twice.
You would hate
that I go right over the rocks you taught me to avoid. My
patterns don't make sense
and if I stop to flip a turtle or watch a baby snake periscope its new
world, I can hear you asking. I can sense your puzzlement.

You told me once: "Lil, if there is an ass-backward way to do
something you will find it." I smile, remembering running
down the up escalator in the Paris Metro—you catching me in time
for the free concert in Saint Sulpice. We made it.
We always made it.

And now I hit the rock and it makes that crunching noise
and now I go over the rock
and over it
and let it make that crunching noise because
something
should be allowed to make noise.

You would hate the way
I keep stopping the mower to get a drink
or write a few lines.

You would hate the way
I go over twigs of increasing size
just to see how much the blades can take.

You would not understand why I keep it in first gear
only.
And only you
would understand why sometimes I mow the lawn more
than once a week.

The Potency of Thought

The potency of thought vibrates—
a sound softer than cracking but louder than reality.
Dreams crowd the safety of oblivion.

The bones of my brain have not yet been picked clean.
There is a dream of you well (and wild) again, and
the potency of thought vibrates.

Musty, mesquite sequences form; opening
past desert nights of wind and warmth and
dreams crowd the safety of oblivion.

But there is a beauty in dreams,
where colors taste like licorice.
The potency of thought vibrates

into the soft, soft sighing of trees.
Un-bitter now,
dreams crowd the safety of oblivion.

An unyielding benevolence storms towards the me
who was us, forcing a taste of the crumbs in my mind while
the potency of thought vibrates with
dreams, crowding the safety of oblivion.

What Is It About Loneliness That Tastes So Good?

It smells like sea salt and vomit yet we love it like it was Swiss chocolate. And here comes Serendipity in her full naked glory, taking the place of any *planned* sorrow. "Heartbreak is only a heartbeat away," she quips.

There is that elastic moment when the phone rings that will take me either to my love or to a telemarketer from Illinois who wants to GIVE me a condo in Bermuda if I would only . . .

It's about the evening you realize you are pregnant and you'll never be alone again. And nothing is lonelier than that.

It's about the evening you wake (dreaming?) and hear his breath soft as 900-grade sandpaper on clay almost dry enough to fire.
And nowhere is more beautiful than that.

Beethoven's "Für Elise" on a sunny day when you should be outside,
but you want to pretend
it's gray out there—

wine and stale crackers instead of homemade soup—
pillows and books and blankets amidst the decaying smokeair and
dying plants— its elegant flavor on my palate like fine Brie with
caviar—
knowing all the while it's only saltines and yellow
American cheese.
Lonely is an inside movement.

What I Want

I want
more than a red dress
(I've had one or two).
I want severance pay for time served.
Memorial Sloan Kettering Cancer Center
can validate my parking.
I want the ends to justify the means,
and I want healthy chocolate.

I want to rub the bottle of cabernet like a genie's lamp
and watch you appear. You've traveled to stranger places.

I want to stop dreaming that you are still alive.
I want to *never* stop dreaming that you are still alive.

I want to sleep later and longer to shorten my time here—
this place where you are not,
but were.

I want that sexy spot of in-between
(when your leg shakes you almost awake but not quite)
to last longer. This hypnagogic jerk
is not as involuntary as it sounds.

I want people to stop asking me if I am ready to move
on.

Move like a pawn, a little at a time?
Or like an elegant, sweeping queen
across this black and white deathboard? Whether I move
on or above or about or between, beyond, through, or
underneath—
I am still without.

No preposition of wanting
will win this argument of time
and place and space.

I want to stop
wanting.

Peter Pan's Madrigal

You were never meant to stay
rooted to the ground, or even to one country—let alone this plane.
You had a Peter Pan shadow with a luggage tag attached.

Grateful that you taught me (finally) how to play,
our story became one of life untamed.
You were never meant to stay
rooted to the ground, or even to one country—let alone this plane.

Nothing you have given me can be taken away,
but nothing you have given me will ever be the same.
I know by some magic moving against the grain
that you were never meant to stay
rooted to the ground, or even to one country—let alone this plane.
You had a Peter Pan shadow with a luggage tag attached.

Metastasis of a Cancer Cell

I cannot survive
without you.
Do not look so horrified.
Isn't that the cliché you
have always wanted to hear?
All is certainty now, and I
will automatically bind yours to mine,
and make our very cells one. I will enter you. We will fuse.
Conjugation, budding, name your euphemism; I will change
your essence.
I will corrupt your system—invade and destroy
all that is strong and good in you.

Victim, killer, who is who? I am the one who cannot survive
without you. Reprogramming, weakening, I will transform.
What makes you think you can treat me, heal me, abolish me
Wait.
I am fragile without you.
I am unalive without you. I have no walls, no center.
I am genetic instruction inside a shell.
I replicate within you.
I convert you.
I am
You
now.
I thrive.
You starve.

We will end this together.
The We Who Was You cannot fight.
Let us go then, you and I . . .
I am still too small to be seen
too small.

Afterward

My life is now an apostrophe of existence;
absence, a definition of its own.
I finally learned a truth, but
this is mere supposition.

Absence, a definition of its own.
Does existence mark a possession?
This is mere supposition;
what we were is not who we are.

Does existence mark a possession?
It is not possible to love without wonder.
What we were is not who we are,
wrapped in this falsehood of starlight.

It is not possible to love without wonder.
I finally learned a truth, but
wrapped in the falsehood of starlight,
my life is now an apostrophe of existence.

Sestina for My Husband Who Is Not Coming Home

I want to die before I forget
that laughter sustained us before the fear.
The cult of cancer is not gentle.
I am more than hollow; I am incarnate anger.
No religion will have me.
There is no tomorrow that is whole.

Memory cannot make me whole,
as if I could forget
your pain. I wish it had been me.
I guess people say that out of fear,
lest they be thought lucky rather than admit anger.
Oh, our lost life. It was dazzling. It was gentle.

The travels themselves may not have all been gentle,
but the homecomings were majestic and whole.
Poison's liquid anger
couldn't save you any more than I could forget
you charming nurses into midnight cigarette forays. You: no fear.
I could deny you nothing. Not me.

And as for me,
time is not gentle
like some say. My constant fear
is not dying yet. I can't be made whole.
Sometimes I forget
that you are not on a trip, and so returns the anger.

I wonder if without anger
the September breezes would speak to me
of something other than loss. I forget
that you are not coming home, and the remembering is not gentle.
There is nothing to be afraid of now. The whole
is certainly not the sum of its parts without fear.

There is no more fear,
only anger
and the lacerations of my heart. A whole
world away, in a lifetime long ago, there was you and me
and kitchen dancing gentle
as grief. Time does not forget.

If there is no fear,
then there is no hospital for you or me.
If there is no you, then all I have is anger.
There is not much in life that is gentle.
But taken as a whole,
there will always be an *us* I do not forget.

Saturday Poetry Workshop: What Have You Learned?

I learned . . . that a huge weight lifted off my shoulders just moves
to land hard on my heart.

I wish I felt empty.

I learned that time moves according to memory
and not the other way around.

I could say I learned how
to navigate the miasma of hospitals and jargon and cancer but—
anyone can learn that.

I learned that the diagnostic differential is really what they call it—
just like on T.V.

I learned that a stranger with a mop in one hand
covering me with our worn Mexican blanket as I slept on the final
chair-bed next to you
is what finally made me cry.

Symmetry of Loss

Remembering means living inside a prayer.
I would bend the tides,
scarify the light,
castrate the Moon's shadowed dim,
to trust what I can barely feel.
My heart fractures at the inevitable lack of response.

But, an absence of response
doesn't silence the prayer.
To evoke *is* to feel;
pain is inevitable as tides.
I welcome the dim—
never wail in the light.

Reminiscence isn't meant for daylight.
I need a dark response;
mornings are still dim
as the possibility of prayer.
The cold honesty of ocean tides
grants the power to feel.

Pain's thoughtless drudgery feels
unworthy of light.
But I cannot ignore the tides,
the relentless agony of call and response.
I offer another prayer
unheard in the dim.

I moan, I weep in the dim
to stretch my forgetting, to feel
anything other than the missing pieces of a prayer.
If I could hide inside the light—
but an ancestral response
would speak only of tides.

This paradox of tides:
inexorable, yet shifting in the dim,
does not offer a response.
I am doomed to feel
memories of the light,
and be content with ineffectual prayer.

The symmetry of tides, of prayer,
is only a vestigial response to light.
The dim's cold repose is all I can feel.

The Suitcase

It rolls toward me
across the old floor
as if to say, "Take *me!*"

I know where everything goes,
how it all fits. Rolled-up dresses,
sandals for beach, sandals for walking.

And a book I haven't read but
meant to
a long time ago.

My hair won't tolerate
a brush, so I don't bring one
just in case you've forgotten yours.

You made a game of overpacking, but
if I've used everything I brought,
it's a win.

As I zip it up, I think
of the pock marks rain makes
in the sand

that my footsteps
will smooth
out.

Stomping My Foot

I want to channel some of this horror into poetry.

I want to be the wife
who makes everything better; magically,
like Samantha twitching her nose.
In a black and white world
this might be possible.

Too much color here.
Red blood, white needles, cerulean walls,
silver elevators, barely blue chairbeds,
burnt umber striped fish in the tank
of the chemo suite waiting room—give me back
my three channels; a simple flag song,
our preamble to static. Give me back.

Give me back the world
of Mexican beaches
and the two of us dancing
alone
late at night
before bed.

I am selfish.
I should want cures,
and peace in the Middle East,
an end to poverty, and more room
in the Ronald McDonald House;
and I should want people to start
using adverbs again.

But I am selfish.
Selfish and stuck
between synonymous pages:
need, and desire.

II

Mothers' Advice

This is a world of war,
this big blue speck of dust
looping through the void.

We've been at war
since before you were born.
Of course, we can't see it.
These wars are not on television,
not since Vietnam.
They've learned.
Images persist.

Images persist,
and we must choose
to save the elephants
or the Alaskan wilderness
or the hurricane-ravaged countries of people
or the earthquake-ravaged countries of people
or the hungry. These choices we make.

This holiday season I will give
a goat to Ethiopia in your name.
Wrapping isn't eco-friendly anyway.

This is a world of change,
this big blue dot, this holy mother,
this flying rock of carbon-happy creatures.

We lift up the daughters.
We honor the feminine in each of us;
until these lines,
the yin-yang, the black-white—
these analytical demarcations,
will be erased in time.

Birth is painful.
No one wants to wake up
here.
Easy isn't always good,
and equal
does not mean fair.
Images persist.

Images persist,
and we must choose
to feel the breath of fog,

and the needles of sleet
and the meandering light across evergreens
and the dull throb of sunsets
and the insistence of connection.
This is faith.
This is the cascade
of hope.

Tree roots are only
invisible
if we don't look down.
Bears and rosebuds
are always here,
even in the snow-depths,
if we see with time.

Grape Skin

We are outside drinking from the hose. My younger sister Heidi and I are squelching our toes in the wet grass. Usually, we'd get yelled at for wasting water but everyone else is inside yelling about something else.

We distract ourselves by picking grapes and sucking the rich flesh from their skin and spitting the seeds at each other. The hose runs, cleans us off. Squelching our toes in the wet grass, we are hidden by the open door to the cellar. If we need to, we can run down there to hide.

Summer threatens us;
freedom to, not freedom from
drinking from the hose.

Where Is Ophelia's Mother?

Ophelia had her hands full when you
think about it. How many men can one
woman please? Daddy, lover, brother—too
much testosterone for a girl so young.

Who were her role models? Gertrude? Whore
or innocent, however you view her
she is black and white, and a girl needs more
shades to learn truth; that sisterlove is near.

Ophelia's frustrated voice is heard
centuries later, yet here we still drown.
Without the mother, the lines are too blurred.
Remembering in wombs alive, girls born,
forgetting. Why can't we dream them stronger?
Where is her mother? Today, only anger.

Likenesses

In this mirror, my face is a wolf, teeth bared.
In another mirror, my face is a footstep in the sand.

Looking into the lake I see a lily-pad corsage.
Looking into the ocean's tide pools I see
a graying mermaid's laughter.

There is a smoky, blurred image of a girl looking back at me
from a subway window
from a long time ago.

Go further back and there is a child on tiptoe looking at the
bathroom mirror asking, "Why am I here? Why?"

Later, the child knows without asking why the bathroom mirrors in
this place are glued to the wall, unbreakable.

Later, because she can see her reflection in the creek water below,
she knows the bridge is not high enough.

Later, she says *yes* so often she forgets their questions.
And no one tells her that what she is asking
cannot be found in the back seat with her jeans around her ankles.

In this mirror, my face is a wolf, teeth bared.
In this mirror, the child looks back, feral. She cannot see me.
Not yet.

Sonnet for the Girls

Miranda, Ophelia, and Lady M:
I wandered through your dialogue aching
for mother answers, or sisters to condemn.
I found only men, only men taking.

Alone in a swamp of truth, I cringed.
But inside your words, there! Another place.
On the magic of this stage, I paraded,
only to find an angry queen in mirror's face.

Going back to your visions; betrayal,
revenge, oh I learned to dream the big one.
You taught me who we are; we are not frail.
So, so young I read your lives—coming undone.
If only I could send a Mother's Day card
to all my girls to say it won't be so hard.

Forgive Me, But I Wasn't Feeling So Civil

Civil discourse used to prevent me from saying, "pussy."
Now that it's out in the open, let's open it up. Fierce daughters
dream of agency and justice, as well as ponies.

We've been pushed down too far to not show our pink.

Civility is respect for fellow human beings.
The violence of words is measured in blood, not in a lexicon
of skirted euphemisms trying not to show their doublespeak
(the hemlines—please!).

This one and only race is . . . just that.

Civilized dialogue is crucial to empathy.
Who are we if not the stories we bear, the imaginings of possibility,
the abstract constructions we call a philosophy?

Moving only in straight lines will kill us all.

Civilization is an advancement of more than cutlery.
Extraction of pearls isn't as peaceful as it sounds,
not for the oyster.
The conservation of matter is an equation that will balance,
unintended or not.

We are our children's mirrors.

Civilians cannot be silent noncombatants, not anymore, not now.
There is a war of compassion going on. Kill with kindness? You
have not tamed the shrew; you've taught her.

Bear witness to the ferocity of tears.

On Seeing the Pietà

Her gentle face,
eyelids crushed forever downward, holds in
the gasping sob that is her heart.
One hand wrapped, one hand questioning,
she breathes from the womb.

No thought is left.
It is only desire and death,
as always.
Merciful pity, if one could be so redundant,
has left no words for the mouth or mind—only salt.

Mary, your folds envelop so much more
than your son.
You are the eternal lap.
A vestigial icon of femaleness,
how many goddesses died as whores to make room for you?

How many crones cried for the death
of blood as birth?
As power?
Your sheer spiritual circumference
brings my tears.

Marble majesty,
did he cry as he found you
underneath the chisel sound?
Did he know
who he unearthed?

You are of stone.
You are of splendor.
You, mother of all
mothers,
are my secret pagan queen.

Rule of Thumb

This life is a gentle one
if you walk a foot behind the men.
A world is coming undone.

Teach your daughters: wear claws and run,
or stay in the predator's pen.
This life is a gentle one?

Rape not a hate crime? *What* then? A hit and run?
She was wearing what? Well, then . . .
That world is coming undone.

He didn't mean anything by it; it was just for fun,
locker room talk again.
His life is a gentle one.

Girls, this is old hand. Close your mouth. Cut and run.
A scar is a scar is a scar, now and then.
This world is coming undone.

Unleash words. Destroy the *hush,* let's run
loose in the night as in the day again—
this life is a gentle one.

Their world will come undone.

On Magritte's *The Voice of Blood*

Art evokes the mystery without which the world would not exist
—René Magritte

I think we should listen more to
old wives and their tales.

Learn how not to get caught in a storm
(of fear),
not to enter the (wrong)
doors,
how to avoid the falling
stars (or catch a ride).

How to let go (and know)
when trees are silent they are free.

The voice of blood is captured in the geometry
of trees and the lie of open windows.
Meandering grays bend in moonlight's
fortune-telling whispers.
Listen.
There is no color without light.

Listen
to the moonlight shape our
monochromatic truth.

Listen, old wives,
to our prayers for fairytale endings ever,
ever,
after.

Gray is washed in morning
graffiti of the light revealed.

Not If, But When

Women: tweet me your first assaults, they aren't just stats. I'll go first:
Old man on city bus grabs my "pussy" and smiles at me. I'm 12.
    —Kelly Oxford (@kellyoxford) October 7, 2016; 7:48 p.m. Tweet

She didn't ask if; she asked when.
There were thousands of replies in the first hour. There were over a
million in the first 24.

> *I was four the first time. I remember because I wasn't in*
> *school yet.*

Not *If . . .* but *When.*

No one notices *If* sitting in the corner. *If* is small and dark and
blends in. *If* waits.

When doesn't need to hide.
When is the flagellation of inevitability.

I didn't know it was called rape. I thought all twelve-year-olds said
yes. It made me special. What was there to tell?

> *I was eleven, and it wasn't rape really . . .*

Meanwhile, a bunched-up pair of panties, blood of inner thighs,
mountains and mountains of skulls from girlhood are tossed into
the past and as forgotten as the tooth left for the fairy. It's a rite of
passage.

At breakfast, three women share rape stories. One woman is silent.
That doesn't mean she doesn't have a story.

I was already fifteen so I don't know if it counts . . .
He said I was his very own "little girl."
I never told anyone—I was ashamed.
He said he would kill me.
He said he loved me.
It was my fault.
I was drunk.
I . . .

And we sigh
and we share
and we shrug
and we are silent.

Frozen screams line up in collective memory as if they
belonged there.

This is not normal.
Is this not normal?

Not *If* but . . . When. *When?*

I want *When* out of the driver's seat. I want *When* chained by the
neck, running with cracked, bleeding feet behind the car.

What of mercy?

He said, "Just touch it. We don't have to do anything."

Canis Lupus

The males are comparatively laid back, sorting out their status through threats and bluff. The females draw blood.

—Living with Wolves

I fought for Alpha, bled and tore her flesh.
Mythologies debunked: I couldn't care
any less about a full moon. I howl
whenever brothers, sisters sing; I sing.
I mate for power, not for life. If he
does weaken, die, I choose another male.
I'll die . . . to protect my pups, our future.
Nibbling faces of the pack, I love hard.

I lick the blood from your wounds;
I lick the blood from my womb;
I lick the blood from our kill;
I lick the blood from my lips.
Fierce in my invocations, joyful in
loyalty, I teach our pups to begin.

Deep End of Instinct

Calling to Baba Yaga, not running away, does she dream of waves?
Enter primeval bold sisterhood, a salty, turbulent scream of waves.

Triple Goddesses' spiral: a Maiden, a Mother, a Crone, speech past
Father Time, dusty contrivance too linear. Beams of waves.

Crying womb memory, poets elaborate story dimensions, while
passing a history through tears, a sorrow song gleams of waves.

Languages ancient, so old *La Llorona*'s forgotten, are fire's tears.
Silent absorption of lessons, these words, tidal, the reams of waves.

Fracture the darknesses, Poet; ancestral vision escapes it all.
Into the instinct, the deep end of instinct, caress of waves.

Ocean

Standing here, rocking
with the swells,
I feel both the terror
and tenderness—
wildness
of the womb.
This is as close
as I get to prayer.
Rip current rivers
kill faster if
you fight them.
She is at least
four billion
years old,
our mother.
As soon as she
got enough oxygen, she
gave us birth.
She turns stone
to dust.
Deception is the nature of waves.

Drink Me

Shrinking like Alice, the coneflower, purple-soft,
towers above me. It welcomes bees, butterflies.
Mother plant, edible petals, a giver.

Marvelous honeybees thudding out music like
furry-fat airplanes. Alive in harmonious
singing, I somehow know, growing again, I don't—

cannot—belong with them. Hummingbirds buzz me, and
comfort me. Giant as I am again, no more deafening
than my heartbeat.

Particle Song

The particle song is a lullaby to permanence.
These mountains: soft, green, curved,
are not our Sonoran mesas—dusted red angles, a haven
for creation.

But I am learning contemplation as the summer is tucked in.
I was never good at bedtime story-songs, so as I try and write
a poem about these eastern volcanic remnants, I hear instead
the promise of waves to the sand.

The promise of death to us all.

Only particles connect our dots.
How massive and microscopic, these tectonics that bind us.

I was trying to write a poem about these mountains
but I heard you,
and cannot help but sing this love song to permanence instead.

A Poem for Dirt

I would love to write about winter rain and gloaming and sunrise happy mornings, or the spring smells of bulbs cracking through thawed surfaces.

Admittedly, however, the nostalgic smell of diesel fuel carries my images and metaphors. Windblown hair on stormy streetlight nights, ducking through life anonymously, peacefully.

When I think of dirt I think of worms and birds eating them and of cats eating birds, coyotes eating cats wondering if *people* really eat cats, thinking, how odd that there is no one to eat us.

Feeding dirt, raindrops are for dancing along car windows
and train windows, furiously trying to escape the inevitable.
Like being eaten by the sun.

Rain turns nakedly to ice crystals, powerful as hammers. Or water warm, carried in cells of porous membranes—we are fluid. Floating then ripped from the liquid. No wonder babies cry.
It's the transience that terrifies.

Crepuscular awakenings itching like late afternoon coffee, or like cocktails before noon; the outer edge of fury and remorse, dusk is my favorite.

Glowtime. When even silver halide produces beauty in negative. Light caresses rusty metal, turning junk into treasure in time for it to disappear for the bats' arrival. Alive in the in-between, watching them dart around quiets me.

It's all a ball of dirt. The warming smell of fresh green shoots, the seemingly sacrificial mounds of chipmunks, the watery mix that dresses cars with brown spotted lace—all, all are life and dirt.

At sunrise when the first moments of awareness stab like gentle acupuncture needles, I wander through the envelope of our embrace before I try and imagine how many times this has already happened

in todays all over the world.

Dinner

There is a magnificent spider living in a grand web above my grill
and as hungry as I am for flesh, if I light the grill she will die
and if I shake her off she will be hurt, homeless,

and she is not the beautiful dragonfly
who chose to expire on your houseplant,
but she is strangely fabulous and I love her somehow.

To make a new web!—this so shimmeringly full of deathlife.
I do not wish it on her. Abundantly full and fat and hairy
she knows nothing of my deliberations, of my dilemma.

I have shucked corn, and water is boiling.
I have sat and smoked
and filled my wine glass.

I am afraid to move her,
and I am afraid to light the grill.
The consequence is mine.

The exquisite bats begin
their nightly dance for food, and still
I wait.

How long does a spider live?
If I knew she were Charlotte I could be Wilbur.
But how often? For how long?

And where are her children?
Before I pour another glass of wine
and eat her myself out of pure, vampiric condolence,

I should make the salad.
I should light the fireplace.
I should believe I have an answer.

III

Why We Are Here

Why can't we wonder about what . . .
is?
Is it too close to us, this magnificent reality of existence?

We focus on the destiny of starlight, the dank history of gravity.
We invite wars to decide who deserves to live
and whose sacred text to read.
We debate whether or not robots and clones and AIs are human;
we string together "what ifs" like a necklace or
a noose.

We write books (and then read them) about our purpose in life,
our destiny; our inner dialogue with free will chatters on for
decades and
is it not—
is it not enough
to know that the first sound every human being hears is the
orchestra of the womb?
The mother's beating heart, air moving in and out of her lungs,
even the sound of her blood moving through the umbilical cord.

Is it not enough
of a miracle that every human being shares 99% of their DNA
with
every
other
human being?

We can transfer a living human heart from one body to the next;
we can print a heart from a machine. But we don't know
why we laugh, or why cats purr.

We know that black holes can swallow entire stars—that the
Magnus Effect makes balls fly instead of fall.

Why not wonder why the gray of a rainy autumn afternoon is
different that the gray of a snowstorm?

We don't stop
in astonishment at the ray of sunlight caressing a child's face, or
the graceful power of hummingbird flight.

We want a reason for our objective reality,
and then we want to argue about it.

And all the while there is the tender blue of morning and the
raging violets of evening and the scars of our individual little
lives all
waiting, waiting for us to see.

Listen

Let them collapse like paper dolls in the rain, these fears.
Screams are not howls and not cries—all is echo,
echo of scavenged tears.

Mythologies transparent as jellyfish and just as deadly
writhe in the corners of our thoughts
if we allow them. Their sounds, a gruesome medley.

We gulp our madness down like shots
instead of sipping the bigger story.
This is how history plots.

But there is a tale ancient as breath
that whispers to us all.
In this version, the happily ever after is ours
if we can hear her song through clouded stars.

Postcard to the Dead

I remember rescue from life's dull deluge—
spoonsful, tiny, memory road trips; beauty
now attentive, energy gently faithful,
through your eyes, always.

Once upon . . . imagine us raising, holding
Time aloft and building our coastal castle.
Listen: wave laps, rhythmic purrs, wind-howls
gathering shadows.

Here There Be Dragons

On reading Citizen: An American Lyric *by Claudia Rankine*

"She never actually saw you sitting

there."

> Were you?

> There?

What passes for essence? What . . . passes?

> You are your own enigma caught inside the net of the other.
> caught inside the glass-ceilinged portal
> caught living in your own head

> caught.

Who is there to talk to when the corruption of emptiness takes
hold?

> When you find your heart sitting

> alone . . . in the dark . . . smoking and
> drinking and staring

at a blank
screen—it has given up trying to

inhabit the tension of language.

Noise

The catalpa leaves are naked
in this light.
A bird and a squirrel fighting
for a plot of limb
in a rage
of Discordia.

Stabs of vertical white
bouncing off the translucent hummingbird feeder
blinds me,
and it's almost soundless.

I was trying to write a poem about the futility of war,
but blazoned on the red clay pot full
of dying basket flowers is a *slap*
of contrast. Behind it, rope hammock
backlit with a sonata.

There is a lullaby going on
by my feet; the deck's
cedar grains and knots are soothing a thick band
of ambered light.
Or maybe it's the other way around.

Halyomorpha halys, also known
as the brown marmorated stinkbug, bumbles
along the glass table.
His reflection is whistling.

Bright refracted rectangles are joining
with the unmown lawn in a green-lit duet.

     If wind had a color, would it be white?
     If we could translate howling, would it be song?

This cacophony of sunlight
distracts me.

Once things quiet down out here, I'll get back to work.

By House

I have lived in this house before I ever saw this house.
I have dreamed of this house only while awake.
By house I mean property, by property I mean buildings red and
weathered, gorgeoused by the sunlight in their abandonment
and decrepitude.
By house I mean dogs in green thick grass and deer at twilight.
By house I mean trees; trees so old you could climb up and
live in one where no one could find you.
By house I mean a sky of lightning bolts and thunder treacherous
as the idea of gods.
By house I mean rocking chair outdoors—nothing about this house
is trapped indoors.
By house I mean home.

Topology

First, the bedroom where you died. I sleep on the couch downstairs instead of a hotel because that's what you would do, and now I need to figure out what I would do, but I still can't make big decisions like light fixtures or closets.

White walls please. Space to hang his art.
The other rooms upstairs? Sure. Might as well.
Knock down the walls and see what's there.

I buy the Mexican tile for the new bathroom, made full by a shower. I order the Talavera sink because you would love it, love it like our desert days in spaces open and western wild. I straddle the past with the now because the future isn't visible yet. I know it will go on without me. The building does. Insulation, drywall, flooring, windows new and tight to let only light in—not cold. No breeze, like hospital rooms, all the hospital rooms. So, I open them wide. Wide enough for you to get in if you need to, my Peter Pan.

The house grows; home shrinks
from your death. A point in space,
habitat only.

November

Lake Michigan looms
outside the frost and fog.

Don't worry. You don't need to have been to Michigan
to see it.

Picture that gleeful bastard—Winter—chasing
Demeter underground, Persephone waiting in sweatpants and
a pomegranate-stained hoodie.

Picture
blue-glazed water, cold enough to kill.

Picture tardy geese frozen in place.
You don't need to go there to see it.

Picture
the tomorrow
of our discontent—we
chink, chink, chink with our icepicks of art
to free one stupid goose.

And it matters to that one.
It matters.

I Am Picking Buttercups

I am picking buttercups, those
worn-out childhood weeds.

Persistent as grass, they
flail toward uncertainty every
single year.

Don't worry—those are sweat tears.
I don't cry
in front of beauty
if I can help it.

White daisies and red roses together
are my favorite.
Blooming at the same time,
if they had fingers, they would—in unison—stick up
the middle ones.

Sell a dozen of these, said the daisy.
Pull me up only to toss me out, says the rose.

Desert

In vast silences
of sunrise,
I have found the pillow
that smells like I do.

Oceanic views of
mountain saddles
bring me close, closer
to who I was
when I first asked.

Discordant howls
soothe sleepless hours
remembering
roaming,
wild running—
in packs.

Alone now,
in this incongruous solitude
of faces, memory past,
forgotten visions urge me
to embrace cloudless skies:
the ephemeral oneness of
earthsky and windfire.

I am home here,
in violent sounds of morning.

There Is No Color Without Light

I

Painting square chips
of color
matching the hue—
just so—to their commercial
counterparts, Vermilion
is a real challenge.

A bit more black
moves toward
Crimson. A bit more
white,
bright
as Scarlet.

Take your chips into the closet;
test them!

There, in the
windowless space,
all is gray,
varying shades
of gray,
an infinite number of grays.

II

In the predawn
moments before
the world
turns on, the reality
of gray rules.

Hidden from final
vestiges of moonlight,
hunted by dawn,
I bend toward
the only light I know.

A soggy awakening
made not of time
but of torment.
Cracks emerge.
I triage

the duality,
the rise
and fall
of light.

III

Graced
as we are
by the death
of stars,

I want only
to burst back into
atoms of death.

A laconic resonance
takes precedence,
and I embrace
this triptych of shades:

darkness, grayness, light—
a pretense
of care
or custody.

The hues of time
are cruel. Know,
beyond it all,
beneath the coveted
autumnal color
and the brazen
burning yellows

of daybreak,
the truth
of gray.

Night Shift

On Alexis Rhone Fancher's Waiting

Softer than Hopper's *Nighthawks,*
my greys
unfold nightmares and day
dreams of coffee can cash,
rolling quarters,
spilling time.

Luscious and fluid,
my shifts
release harmonies into the
cacophony
of survival.

The dollar pinned to the wall
was not my first.

Forever is illusory.

Watching Saint Sebastian

Saint Sebastian
Andrea Mantegna c. 1480

You look, poor pin cushioned saint, as if
you are about to make a run for it.
Mantegna has shown you with just a little blood—a pinprick
if you will.

Rosy-cheeked, looking up at the decay in dismay
I can see you asking, "Why?"

The two on the bottom right have not yet decided
whether you need a new incision. As if the arrows
were of some outrageous fortune and not the slings of faith.

A sneaky soldier, you had the best of intentions. Pray and comfort
prisoners in secret. Wear the brandishments of your enemy
and pretend.

You are my favorite saint. Your sin was not deceit,
but getting caught.

Few tourists standing in awe of your pain know
you did not die tied
and picked at and poked.
You returned to have your enemy beat you to death instead.

Label Me Human

I will fill in the circle for "other"
and write my country of origin as Earth.

Spread the word—
all human beings share 99%
of their DNA with
each other. We are one race;
this is science: an unwritten
entitlement to humanity.

"We" is more than a pro-noun.
It is a pro-nounce-ment.
There is no otherness
inherent in a fetus,
or a poem.

Yin and Yang do not stand
on opposite sides of the street
in protest. The greatest deceit
is that we are separate;
in this societal simulation
no one is real, but

we are not artificial
intelligence;
we *are* the real deal, we who make
Art and dance in kitchens.

Tell me what I cannot say,
and I will infest you with words.

Tell me who I cannot be,
and I will rip open my chest—
show you my heart.

Perception Recipe

An awareness of all-ness feeds me
nourishes the parts of me left dry
by things. The thing-ness of snow
is potentially
treacherous and must be fought.

The all-ness of snow
is the magic of water
meeting particle—a merging crystallization
of beauty.

Add winter sunlight, blend gently, and
we have Art.

Nibbles of starlight
sprinkled along the edges of a
pastry moon,
galactic darkness—

I am not apart
from
this.

Of Light and Mornings

I may go out into the world later.
Now I want to go in
to the outer world.

Diffused distractions
move along the corners of morning, and there's a chipmunk.
Darting in and out of not-so-hidden spaces until
it decides I am no threat.

Refractions and reflections paint the gray out of pre-dawn,
the source moving higher in the sky as I walk. This changes
everything and leaves all as it was before.

Both Snell and Descartes said so, so . . .

The deer looks at me, pretends I am not there. She looks at me
pretends she is not there. If I look close enough
there are fleas and ticks and maybe lice, but if I stay still and
squint, she could be a mother or a bride.

There is a rustling. Given away by sound, what was invisible
is not.

There is no color yet, and it's comforting,
somehow, to know the grayness below.

I stay still, so still,
and let the mosquito land on my tongue.
It's not as easy as it sounds.

Quarantine

Tell me to stay
so I have time to watch
dandelions become a bumblebee feast.

Tell me to stay
inside the innumerable greens
of May afternoons.

Remind me that I miss
the togetherness of tribe;
come, eat, drink, be
with me, with the us
who turn towards each other
like sunflowers in the absence of light.

Tell me to stay
in the stillness.
Watching the clouds' poetic trajectory,
a caesura to memories of possible tomorrows,
I stop at lily of the valley exhalations.

Their tiny, shy bells blasting
an ode to existence.

Tell me to stay
inside the idea of non-distance
at the quantum level.
I breathe in loneliness and exhale hope.

There is a seductive subservience
in staying, so—
tell me to stay
and watch the gloaming
in all four directions,

one for each deep breath
of myself.

Who Gets to Be You Now?

I write from the past to let you know
your devotion to red alert will fade.

What feels selfish now will heal you and remain
righteous and whole.

Your tears will find new purpose.

In my now, the world exists
of the hospital blocks
around East 66th and
above the chemotherapy suite and
under the MRI wing,
across from the nurse's station and
through fear.

I write from the past to let you know
your sky will expand.

This night will give way to a blood-yolk morning.

The size of the sorrow isn't important—
the measure is constant.
Like stars in the wilderness sky, indulgent and exhaustive,
a nebular luminosity sending messages,
looking for the future.

I write from the past to let you know
what once felt extravagant are now mere rations.

The fierceness of pain will expand
and crack your heart beyond blistering,
beyond devastation.
Let anger's intensity relieve the guilt.

I am the past
and cannot embrace you
like a shroud; what will you become?

I write from the past to let you know
there are things I do not know.

How dangerous is comfort?
How tender the awareness of beauty?

Where is there room for more?

Time Traveler

If a woman holds on to this gift of being old while she is young and
young while she is old, she will always know what comes next.
—Dr. Clarissa Pinkola Estés

Too wizened to laugh—belly laugh—when I was young, you
giggled me until I learned.

Too broken—the pieces searching—you
showed me beauty in bits, in fragmented things.

And I—in turn—drew a roadmap for you
to get lost in.

And I—enveloping—warmed you
until you believed it to be true.

We saw our future back when the desert was new.
We knew that together the world could not shake us off
like so many fleas, like she would the non-believers of love.
When, in the darkness, we scratched for glimmers
flames arose just for us, for us alone.

And now—deprived of your body—your
dazzling joy, I must grow young.

And since I—a long time ago—was old,
there is no other direction for me.

Too insistent on time moving only one way,
not everyone can see past my aged outwardness.

Too resistant to inertia, I
look forward to seeing you for the first time, again.

Dear Love,

I was afraid
that when you died,
no one would call me Lily any longer.
They would recall my paper name
and I would become Lisa again, and Lily would die, too.
But I am both
still
here.

I was afraid
that when you died,
I would not be allowed
to wear my wedding ring any longer.
The widow police
would make me remove it
and replace it
with a tattooed black
heart
instead.

But I wear it sometimes.
Things are just things.
A diamond is not a caress,
a band not a night-whisper.

Remember how we danced in starlit arroyos,
on iguana beaches, and in all
of our kitchens?

We danced.

I was afraid
that when you died,

my heart would crack, split, crumble
into broken glass dust. And it did.
But it wouldn't stay that way.
It's like a balloon
that I can fill with air
or with tears. Either way it
bursts
still.

Oh, Love.
You would be so proud of our son.
He has your travel magic
and your love of strong women.
He has your eloquent tenderness.
He has your gratitude
of
first
snowfalls.

You should know that
he, too, will be a father.
You should know
that he loves well,
with ferocity and grace.

I am still afraid, my love.
I am afraid that someday
I will keep the last promise
you asked of me.

About the Author

Lisa St. John is a writer living in the Hudson Valley of upstate New York. Her poetry appears in many journals and anthologies such as *2Elizabeths, Misfit Magazine, The Poet's Billow, The Ekphrastic Review, Light, Entropy Magazine, The Poetry Distillery, Poets Reading the News, Boomer Lit,* and *Chronogram Magazine.* The poem "There Must Be a Science to This" won The Poet's Billow's Bermuda Triangle Contest. "Particle Song" was a finalist for the 2017 Rash Award in Poetry by Broad River Review. Her poem "The Whens of Now" was selected as a finalist for the New Millennium Writings 44th Literary Awards. *Ponderings,* her first chapbook, was published by Finishing Line Press. Lisa's travel articles are published on GoNomad.com. Her memoir excerpt, "I Still Exist," was published by *Grief Digest,* and her essay, "DIY Apocalypse," was published in *Sleet.* Her essay "Of Mothers and Other Demons" appears in *Tales to Inspire: Moonstone Collection Book 2.*

She can be reached at lisachristinastjohn.com.